THIS BOOK BELONGS TO

_____

_____

START DATE

| MONTH | DAY | YEAR |

THE Miracles OF JESUS

SHE READS TRUTH

Nashville, Tennessee

"ONLY MIRACLE IS PLAIN; IT IS IN THE ORDINARY
THAT GROANS WITH THE WEIGHT OF GLORY."

ROBERT FARRAR CAPON

Seeing is not believing.

I ask for miracles all the time. I implore God for snow days, chase after lost causes, and jockey for acclaim. I ask God to change people. I ask Him to change me. And most of all, I ask Him to heal.

The possibility of miracles is such lush fruit to my imagination. It means that anything is possible. God could pop down, give a little nudge, and fix this problem. And when He doesn't, it's confusing. *If He could do a miracle, why doesn't He do one for me?*

In preparing this study, I noticed that Jesus doesn't do miracles on command. He isn't anybody's trick pony. In fact, He blesses those "who do not see, and yet believe" (John 20:29), and He rebukes a generation that "seeks for a sign" (Matthew 12:39).

And, man, I love a good sign. It seems if Jesus were just willing to do a bit of skywriting, all would believe and the world would be saved. It's so much easier to ask for a sign instead of looking to the person of Christ, to hunt after what He can do for us instead of who He is. **His miracles aren't His message, but rather a testament to who He is.** And even those who witnessed His miracles did not necessarily believe.

As we imagined this study on miracles, our team had some grand old arguments over what actually constitutes a miracle of Jesus, and some wonderful realizations over just how many of His miracles are compassionate healing. Taking miracles for what they are—supernatural intervention in the natural world by a loving God—we set out to put together a beautiful and helpful collection of Scripture and insight for you to do your own study.

In this Scripture reading plan, we aim to take a serious look at miracles and what they are. They are a way God makes His presence known on earth. Jesus' miracles gave confirmation, judgment, deliverance, even mercy. And we aim to eschew what they are not: party tricks, or magic for hire. Miracles are a result of Christ's perfect obedience and alignment with the Father, King of heaven and earth. Jesus' miracles aren't about us, but they are for us.

We hope this study of Christ's miracles in Scripture will reveal to you more of the character of God, invite you to know Him better, and beckon you to delight in Him.

Rebecca

Rebecca Faires
MANAGING EDITOR

letters

THE MIRACLES IN FACT ARE A RETELLING IN SMALL LETTERS
OF THE VERY SAME STORY WHICH IS WRITTEN
ACROSS THE WHOLE WORLD IN
LETTERS TOO LARGE FOR SOME OF US TO SEE.

too large

C.S. LEWIS

HOW TO STUDY WITH THE ONLINE COMMUNITY

For added community and conversation, join us in **The Miracles of Jesus** reading plan on the She Reads Truth app or on SheReadsTruth.com—where women from Grand Rapids to Grand Cayman will be reading along with you!

Have a "He" in your life—a brother, father, husband, friend? Invite him to join you by visiting HeReadsTruth.com or the He Reads Truth app, or by picking up the guy version of this book at ShopHeReadsTruth.com.

HOW TO USE THIS BOOK

She Reads Truth is a community of women dedicated to reading the Word of God every day.
The Bible is living and active, breathed out by God, and we confidently hold it higher than anything we
can do or say. This book focuses primarily on Scripture with helpful elements throughout.

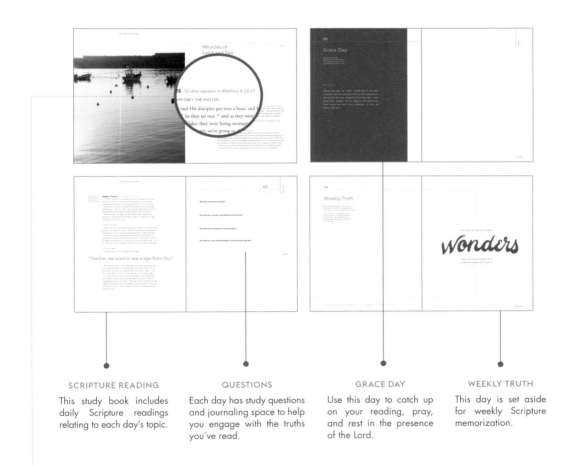

SCRIPTURE READING

This study book includes daily Scripture readings relating to each day's topic.

QUESTIONS

Each day has study questions and journaling space to help you engage with the truths you've read.

GRACE DAY

Use this day to catch up on your reading, pray, and rest in the presence of the Lord.

WEEKLY TRUTH

This day is set aside for weekly Scripture memorization.

Parallel References

The Gospels are the same story told four ways. Many of Jesus' miracles are reported in more than one Gospel. When the miracle is found in the Bible more than once, we have listed those other references with the phrase "also appears in…"

Contents

But Jesus looked at them and said, "With men this is impossible, but with God all things are possible."

MATTHEW 19:26

Miracle: \ˈmir-i-kəl\

(Noun) from the Latin word *miraculum*, **meaning** *wonder*.

1. an historical event or phenomenon which surpasses human or natural power and which cannot be explained by natural or scientific laws, and is therefore considered a display of divine power caused by God

2. a supernatural interference with the natural order of things

What Is
a Miracle?

**An expression
of God's power**

1 Kings 18:20-40

ELIJAH AT MOUNT CARMEL

20 So Ahab summoned all the Israelites and gathered the prophets at Mount Carmel. 21 Then Elijah approached all the people and said, "How long will you hesitate between two opinions? If Yahweh is God, follow Him. But if Baal, follow him." But the people didn't answer him a word.

22 Then Elijah said to the people, "I am the only remaining prophet of the Lord, but Baal's prophets are 450 men. 23 Let two bulls be given to us. They are to choose one bull for themselves, cut it in pieces, and place it on the wood but not light the fire. I will prepare the other bull and place it on the wood but not light the fire. 24 Then you call on the name of your god, and I will call on the name of Yahweh. The God who answers with fire, He is God."

All the people answered, "That sounds good."

25 Then Elijah said to the prophets of Baal, "Since you are so numerous, choose for yourselves one bull and prepare it first. Then call on the name of your god but don't light the fire."

26 So they took the bull that he gave them, prepared it, and called on the name of Baal from morning until noon, saying, "Baal, answer us!" But there was no sound; no one answered. Then they danced, hobbling around the altar they had made.

27 At noon Elijah mocked them. He said, "Shout loudly, for he's a god! Maybe he's thinking it over; maybe he has wandered away; or maybe he's on the road. Perhaps he's sleeping and will wake up!" 28 They shouted loudly, and cut themselves with knives and spears, according to their custom, until blood gushed over them. 29 All afternoon they kept on raving until the offering of the evening sacrifice, but there was no sound; no one answered, no one paid attention.

30 Then Elijah said to all the people, "Come near me." So all the people approached him. Then he repaired the Lord's altar that had been torn down: 31 Elijah took 12 stones—according to the number of the tribes of the sons of Jacob, to whom the word of the Lord had come, saying,

"Israel will be your name"— [32] and he built an altar with the stones in the name of Yahweh. Then he made a trench around the altar large enough to hold about four gallons. [33] Next, he arranged the wood, cut up the bull, and placed it on the wood. He said, "Fill four water pots with water and pour it on the offering to be burned and on the wood." [34] Then he said, "A second time!" and they did it a second time. And then he said, "A third time!" and they did it a third time. [35] So the water ran all around the altar; he even filled the trench with water.

[36] At the time for offering the evening sacrifice, Elijah the prophet approached the altar and said, "Yahweh, God of Abraham, Isaac, and Israel, today let it be known that You are God in Israel and I am Your servant, and that at Your word I have done all these things. [37] Answer me, Lord! Answer me so that this people will know that You, Yahweh, are God and that You have turned their hearts back."

[38] **Then Yahweh's fire fell and consumed the burnt offering, the wood, the stones, and the dust, and it licked up the water that was in the trench. [39] When all the people saw it, they fell facedown and said, "Yahweh, He is God! Yahweh, He is God!"**

[40] Then Elijah ordered them, "Seize the prophets of Baal! Do not let even one of them escape." So they seized them, and Elijah brought them down to the Wadi Kishon and slaughtered them there.

An expression
of God's grace

Psalm 65:5-8

5 You answer us in righteousness,
with awe-inspiring works,
God of our salvation,
the hope of all the ends of the earth
and of the distant seas.
6 You establish the mountains by Your power,
robed with strength.
7 You silence the roar of the seas,
the roar of their waves,
and the tumult of the nations.
8 Those who live far away are awed by Your signs;
You make east and west shout for joy.

An expression
of God's
salvation

Exodus 12:40-42

40 The time that the Israelites lived in Egypt was 430 years. 41 At the end of 430 years, on that same day, all the Lord's divisions went out from the land of Egypt. 42 It was a night of vigil in honor of the Lord, because He would bring them out of the land of Egypt. This same night is in honor of the Lord, a night vigil for all the Israelites throughout their generations.

Exodus 12:51

On that same day the Lord brought the Israelites out of the land of Egypt according to their divisions.

Exodus 14:21-31

21 Then Moses stretched out his hand over the sea. The Lord drove the sea back with a powerful east wind all that night and turned the sea into dry land. So the waters were divided, 22 and the Israelites went through the sea on dry ground, with the waters like a wall to them on their right and their left.

23 The Egyptians set out in pursuit—all Pharaoh's horses, his chariots, and his horsemen—and went into the sea after them. 24 Then during the morning watch, the Lord looked down on the Egyptian forces from the pillar of fire and cloud, and threw them into confusion. 25 He caused their chariot wheels to swerve and made them drive with difficulty. "Let's get away from Israel," the Egyptians said, "because Yahweh is fighting for them against Egypt!"

26 Then the Lord said to Moses, "Stretch out your hand over the sea so that the waters may come back on the Egyptians, on their chariots and horsemen." 27 So Moses stretched out his hand over the sea, and at daybreak the sea returned to its normal depth. While the Egyptians were trying to escape from it, the Lord threw them into the sea. 28 The waters came back and covered the chariots and horsemen, the entire army of Pharaoh, that had gone after them into the sea. None of them survived.

29 But the Israelites had walked through the sea on dry ground, with the waters like a wall to them on their right and their left. 30 That day the Lord saved Israel from the power of the Egyptians, and Israel saw the Egyptians dead on the seashore. 31 When Israel saw the great power that the Lord used against the Egyptians, the people feared the Lord and believed in Him and in His servant Moses.

An expression of God's presence

Exodus 19:16-25

[16] On the third day, when morning came, there was thunder and lightning, a thick cloud on the mountain, and a loud trumpet sound, so that all the people in the camp shuddered. [17] Then Moses brought the people out of the camp to meet God, and they stood at the foot of the mountain. [18] Mount Sinai was completely enveloped in smoke because the Lord came down on it in fire. Its smoke went up like the smoke of a furnace, and the whole mountain shook violently. [19] As the sound of the trumpet grew louder and louder, Moses spoke and God answered him in the thunder.

[20] The Lord came down on Mount Sinai at the top of the mountain. Then the Lord summoned Moses to the top of the mountain, and he went up. [21] The Lord directed Moses, "Go down and warn the people not to break through to see the Lord; otherwise many of them will die. [22] Even the priests who come near the Lord must purify themselves or the Lord will break out in anger against them."

[23] But Moses responded to the Lord, "The people cannot come up Mount Sinai, since You warned us: Put a boundary around the mountain and consider it holy." [24] And the Lord replied to him, "Go down and come back with Aaron. But the priests and the people must not break through to come up to the Lord, or He will break out in anger against them." [25] So Moses went down to the people and told them.

An expression of God's judgment

Exodus 7:3-5

[3] "But I will harden Pharaoh's heart and multiply My signs and wonders in the land of Egypt. [4] Pharaoh will not listen to you, but I will put My hand on Egypt and bring the divisions of My people the Israelites out of the land of Egypt by great acts of judgment. [5] The Egyptians will know that I am Yahweh when I stretch out My hand against Egypt, and bring out the Israelites from among them."

According to today's scriptures, what is a miracle?

How does God use miracles to show:

His power?

His grace?

His salvation?

His presence?

His judgment?

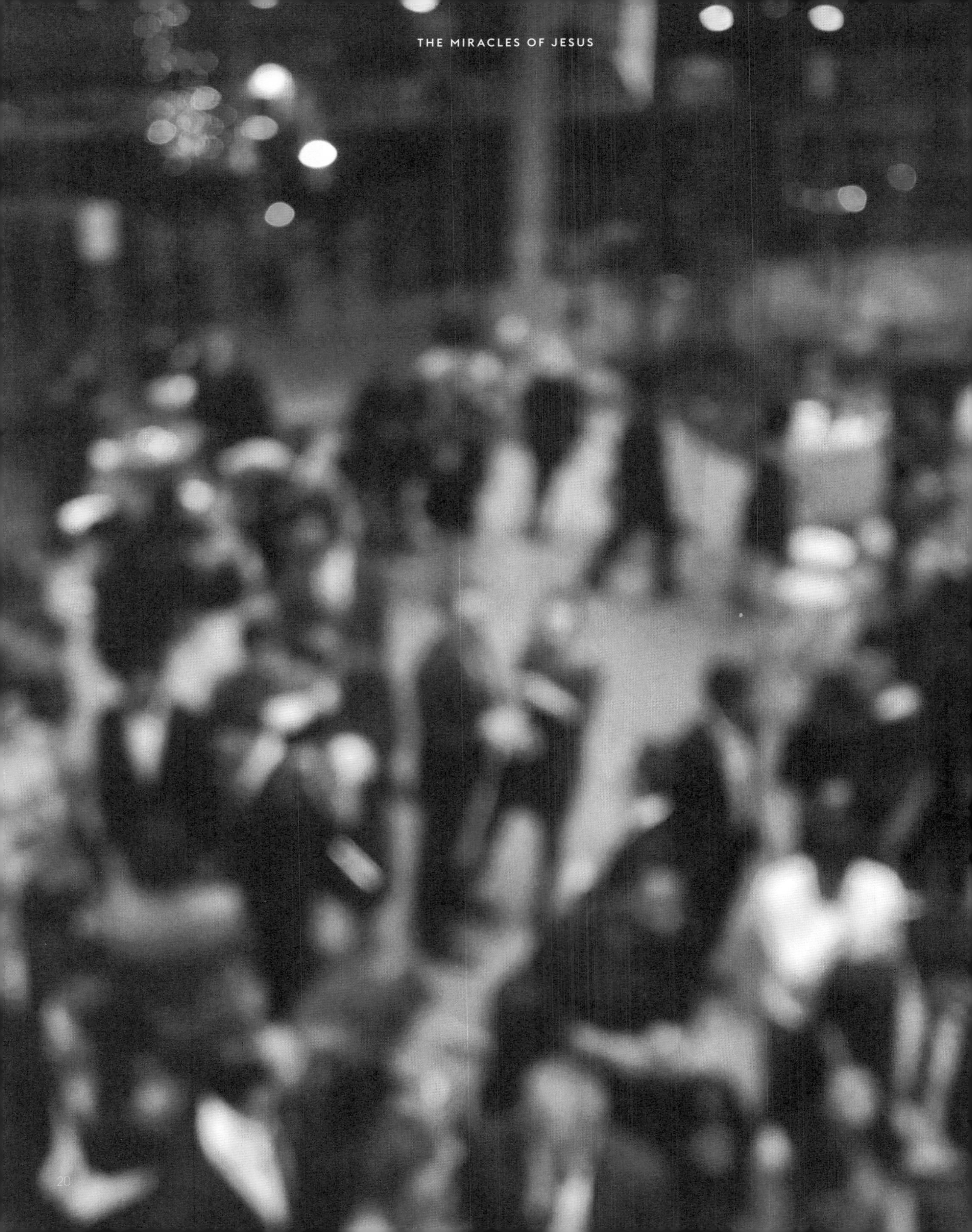

Why Did Jesus Perform Miracles?

To reveal Himself as the Messiah

Matthew 11:2-5

² When John heard in prison what the Messiah was doing, he sent a message by his disciples ³ and asked Him, "Are You the One who is to come, or should we expect someone else?"

⁴ Jesus replied to them, "Go and report to John what you hear and see: ⁵ the blind see, the lame walk, those with skin diseases are healed, the deaf hear, the dead are raised, and the poor are told the good news."

Isaiah 61:1-3

MESSIAH'S JUBILEE

¹ The Spirit of the Lord God is on Me,
because the Lord has anointed Me
to bring good news to the poor.
He has sent Me to heal the brokenhearted,
² to proclaim liberty to the captives
and freedom to the prisoners;
to proclaim the year of the Lord's favor,
and the day of our God's vengeance;
to comfort all who mourn,
³ to provide for those who mourn in Zion;
to give them a crown of beauty instead of ashes,
festive oil instead of mourning,
and splendid clothes instead of despair.
And they will be called righteous trees,
planted by the Lord
to glorify Him.

To reveal His glory

John 2:11

Jesus performed this first sign in Cana of Galilee. He displayed His glory, and His disciples believed in Him.

continued

To show that the Kingdom of God had come with Him

Matthew 12:28-42 📖 *Also appears in Luke 11:29-32*

28 "If I drive out demons by the Spirit of God, then the kingdom of God has come to you. 29 How can someone enter a strong man's house and steal his possessions unless he first ties up the strong man? Then he can rob his house. 30 Anyone who is not with Me is against Me, and anyone who does not gather with Me scatters. 31 Because of this, I tell you, people will be forgiven every sin and blasphemy, but the blasphemy against the Spirit will not be forgiven. 32 Whoever speaks a word against the Son of Man, it will be forgiven him. But whoever speaks against the Holy Spirit, it will not be forgiven him, either in this age or in the one to come.

A TREE AND ITS FRUIT

33 "Either make the tree good and its fruit good, or make the tree bad and its fruit bad; for a tree is known by its fruit. 34 Brood of vipers! How can you speak good things when you are evil? For the mouth speaks from the overflow of the heart. 35 A good man produces good things from his storeroom of good, and an evil man produces evil things from his storeroom of evil. 36 I tell you that on the day of judgment people will have to account for every careless word they speak. 37 For by your words you will be acquitted, and by your words you will be condemned."

THE SIGN OF JONAH

38 Then some of the scribes and Pharisees said to Him,

"Teacher, we want to see a sign from You."

39 But He answered them, "An evil and adulterous generation demands a sign, but no sign will be given to it except the sign of the prophet Jonah. 40 For as Jonah was in the belly of the huge fish three days and three nights, so the Son of Man will be in the heart of the earth three days and three nights. 41 The men of Nineveh will stand up at the judgment with this generation and condemn it, because they repented at Jonah's proclamation; and look—something greater than Jonah is here! 42 The queen of the south will rise up at the judgment with this generation and condemn it, because she came from the ends of the earth to hear the wisdom of Solomon; and look—something greater than Solomon is here!"

Why did Jesus perform miracles?

How did Jesus' miracles reveal Himself as the Messiah?

How did Jesus use miracles to reveal His glory?

How did Jesus show that the Kingdom of God had come with Him?

NOTES

What Do Miracles Teach Us About Jesus?

He is the victorious Lord of all

Colossians 1:15-20

THE CENTRALITY OF CHRIST

[15] He is the image of the invisible God,
the firstborn over all creation.
[16] For everything was created by Him,
in heaven and on earth,
the visible and the invisible,
whether thrones or dominions
or rulers or authorities—
all things have been created through Him and for Him.
[17] He is before all things,
and by Him all things hold together.
[18] He is also the head of the body, the church;
He is the beginning,
the firstborn from the dead,
so that He might come to have
first place in everything.
[19] For God was pleased to have
all His fullness dwell in Him,
[20] and through Him to reconcile
everything to Himself
by making peace
through the blood of His cross—
whether things on earth or things in heaven.

Psalm 77:13-15

[13] God, Your way is holy.
What god is great like God?
[14] You are the God who works wonders;
You revealed Your strength among the peoples.
[15] With power You redeemed Your people,
the descendants of Jacob and Joseph.   *Selah*

He is Lord over creation

Mark 4:35-41

WIND AND WAVE OBEY THE MASTER

[35] On that day, when evening had come, He told them, "Let's cross over to the other side of the sea." [36] So they left the crowd and took Him along since He was already in the boat. And other boats were with Him. [37] A fierce windstorm arose, and the waves were breaking over the boat, so that the boat was already being swamped. [38] But He was in the stern, sleeping on the cushion. So they woke Him up and said to Him, "Teacher! Don't You care that we're going to die?"

[39] He got up, rebuked the wind, and said to the sea, "Silence! Be still!" The wind ceased, and there was a great calm. [40] Then He said to them, "Why are you fearful? Do you still have no faith?"

[41] And they were terrified and asked one another, "Who then is this? Even the wind and the sea obey Him!"

He is the One who overcomes evil

Luke 11:18-23

[18] "If Satan also is divided against himself, how will his kingdom stand? For you say I drive out demons by Beelzebul. [19] And if I drive out demons by Beelzebul, who is it your sons drive them out by? For this reason they will be your judges. [20] If I drive out demons by the finger of God, then the kingdom of God has come to you. [21] When a strong man, fully armed, guards his estate, his possessions are secure. [22] But when one stronger than he attacks and overpowers him, he takes from him all his weapons he trusted in, and divides up his plunder. [23] Anyone who is not with Me is against Me, and anyone who does not gather with Me scatters."

He is the Suffering Servant who bears our infirmities

Matthew 8:14-17

HEALINGS AT CAPERNAUM

[14] When Jesus went into Peter's house, He saw his mother-in-law lying in bed with a fever. [15] So He touched her hand, and the fever left her. Then she got up and began to serve Him. [16] When evening came, they brought to Him many who were demon-possessed. He drove out the spirits with a word and healed all who were sick, [17] so that what was spoken through the prophet Isaiah might be fulfilled:

He Himself took our weaknesses
and carried our diseases.

How do Jesus' miracles show that He is Lord over creation?

What can we learn about Jesus as He overcomes evil?

How does Christ bear our infirmities?

NOTES

Miracles of Food and Drink

Jesus feeds the five thousand

Matthew 14:14-21 📖 *Also appears in Mark 8:1-9*

¹⁴ As He stepped ashore, He saw a huge crowd, felt compassion for them, and healed their sick.

¹⁵ When evening came, the disciples approached Him and said, "This place is a wilderness, and it is already late. Send the crowds away so they can go into the villages and buy food for themselves."

¹⁶ "They don't need to go away," Jesus told them. "You give them something to eat."

¹⁷ "But we only have five loaves and two fish here," they said to Him.

¹⁸ "Bring them here to Me," He said. ¹⁹ Then He commanded the crowds to sit down on the grass. He took the five loaves and the two fish, and looking up to heaven, He blessed them. He broke the loaves and gave them to the disciples, and the disciples gave them to the crowds. ²⁰ Everyone ate and was filled. Then they picked up 12 baskets full of leftover pieces! ²¹ Now those who ate were about 5,000 men, besides women and children.

Jesus causes a huge catch of fish

Luke 5:4-11

⁴ When He had finished speaking, He said to Simon, "Put out into deep water and let down your nets for a catch."

⁵ "Master," Simon replied, "we've worked hard all night long and caught nothing! But at Your word, I'll let down the nets."

⁶ When they did this, they caught a great number of fish, and their nets began to tear.
⁷ So they signaled to their partners in the other boat to come and help them; they came and filled both boats so full that they began to sink.

⁸ When Simon Peter saw this, he fell at Jesus' knees and said, "Go away from me, because I'm a sinful man, Lord!" ⁹ For he and all those with him were amazed at the catch of fish they took, ¹⁰ and so were James and John, Zebedee's sons, who were Simon's partners.

"Don't be afraid," Jesus told Simon. "From now on you will be catching people!" ¹¹ Then they brought the boats to land, left everything, and followed Him.

John 21:1-11

JESUS' THIRD APPEARANCE TO THE DISCIPLES

¹ After this, Jesus revealed Himself again to His disciples by the Sea of Tiberias. He revealed Himself in this way:

² Simon Peter, Thomas (called "Twin"), Nathanael from Cana of Galilee, Zebedee's sons, and two others of His disciples were together.

³ "I'm going fishing," Simon Peter said to them.

"We're coming with you," they told him. They went out and got into the boat, but that night they caught nothing.

⁴ When daybreak came, Jesus stood on the shore. However, the disciples did not know it was Jesus.

⁵ "Men," Jesus called to them, "you don't have any fish, do you?"

"No," they answered.

⁶ "Cast the net on the right side of the boat," He told them, "and you'll find some." So they did, and they were unable to haul it in because of the large number of fish. ⁷ Therefore the disciple, the one Jesus loved, said to Peter, "It is the Lord!"

When Simon Peter heard that it was the Lord, he tied his outer garment around him (for he was stripped) and plunged into the sea. ⁸ But since they were not far from land (about 100 yards away), the other disciples came in the boat, dragging the net full of fish. ⁹ When they got out on land, they saw a charcoal fire there, with fish lying on it, and bread.

¹⁰ "Bring some of the fish you've just caught," Jesus told them. ¹¹ So Simon Peter got up and hauled the net ashore, full of large fish—153 of them. Even though there were so many, the net was not torn.

Jesus turns water into wine

John 2:1-11

THE FIRST SIGN: TURNING WATER INTO WINE

¹ On the third day a wedding took place in Cana of Galilee. Jesus' mother was there, and ² Jesus and His disciples were invited to the wedding as well. ³ When the wine ran out, Jesus' mother told Him, "They don't have any wine."

⁴ "What has this concern of yours to do with Me, woman?" Jesus asked.

"My hour has not yet come."

⁵ "Do whatever He tells you," His mother told the servants.

⁶ Now six stone water jars had been set there for Jewish purification. Each contained 20 or 30 gallons.

⁷ "Fill the jars with water," Jesus told them. So they filled them to the brim. ⁸ Then He said to them, "Now draw some out and take it to the chief servant." And they did.

⁹ When the chief servant tasted the water (after it had become wine), he did not know where it came from—though the servants who had drawn the water knew. He called the groom ¹⁰ and told him, "Everyone sets out the fine wine first, then, after people have drunk freely, the inferior. But you have kept the fine wine until now."

¹¹ Jesus performed this first sign in Cana of Galilee. He displayed His glory, and His disciples believed in Him.

Why did Jesus feed the group of more than five thousand people?

Why was catching fish so meaningful to the disciples?

Why did Jesus turn water into wine? Why was He reluctant to perform this miracle?

NOTES

Miracles of Land and Sea

Jesus calms
the storm

Luke 8:22-25 📖 *Also appears in Matthew 8:23-27*

WIND AND WAVE OBEY THE MASTER

²² One day He and His disciples got into a boat, and He told them, "Let's cross over to the other side of the lake." So they set out, ²³ and as they were sailing He fell asleep. Then a fierce windstorm came down on the lake; they were being swamped and were in danger. ²⁴ They came and woke Him up, saying, "Master, Master, we're going to die!" Then He got up and rebuked the wind and the raging waves. So they ceased, and there was a calm. ²⁵ He said to them, "Where is your faith?"

They were fearful and amazed, asking one another, "Who can this be? He commands even the winds and the waves, and they obey Him!"

Jesus walks
on water

Mark 6:47-52 📖 *Also appears in Matthew 14:22-32*

⁴⁷ When evening came, the boat was in the middle of the sea, and He was alone on the land. ⁴⁸ He saw them being battered as they rowed, because the wind was against them. Around three in the morning He came toward them walking on the sea and wanted to pass by them. ⁴⁹ When they saw Him walking on the sea, they thought it was a ghost and cried out; ⁵⁰ for they all saw Him and were terrified. Immediately He spoke with them and said, "Have courage! It is I. Don't be afraid." ⁵¹ Then He got into the boat with them, and the wind ceased. They were completely astounded, ⁵² because they had not understood about the loaves. Instead, their hearts were hardened.

Jesus summons the fish with the coin in its mouth

Matthew 17:24-27

PAYING THE TEMPLE TAX

[24] When they came to Capernaum, those who collected the double-drachma tax approached Peter and said, "Doesn't your Teacher pay the double-drachma tax?"

[25] "Yes," he said.

When he went into the house, Jesus spoke to him first, "What do you think, Simon? Who do earthly kings collect tariffs or taxes from? From their sons or from strangers?"

[26] "From strangers," he said.

"Then the sons are free," Jesus told him. [27] "But, so we won't offend them, go to the sea, cast in a fishhook, and take the first fish that you catch. When you open its mouth you'll find a coin. Take it and give it to them for Me and you."

Jesus curses the fig tree and it withers

Mark 11:12-14 📖 *Also appears in Matthew 21:18-22*

THE BARREN FIG TREE IS CURSED

[12] The next day when they came out from Bethany, He was hungry. [13] After seeing in the distance a fig tree with leaves, He went to find out if there was anything on it. When He came to it, He found nothing but leaves, because it was not the season for figs. [14] He said to it, "May no one ever eat fruit from you again!" And His disciples heard it.

Mark 11:20-25

THE BARREN FIG TREE IS WITHERED"

[20] Early in the morning, as they were passing by, they saw the fig tree withered from the roots up. [21] Then Peter remembered and said to Him, "Rabbi, look! The fig tree that You cursed is withered."

[22] Jesus replied to them, "Have faith in God. [23] I assure you: If anyone says to this mountain, 'Be lifted up and thrown into the sea,' and does not doubt in his heart, but believes that what he says will happen, it will be done for him. [24] Therefore I tell you, all the things you pray and ask for—believe that you have received them, and you will have them. [25] And whenever you stand praying, if you have anything against anyone, forgive him, so that your Father in heaven will also forgive you your wrongdoing."

With what did Jesus calm the storm on the Sea of Galilee? What does this show us about Jesus?

Why did Jesus walk on water in Mark 6?

Why did Jesus curse the fig tree?

NOTES

Miracles at a Glance

A flyover of Jesus' miracles recorded in the Gospels.*

PRIMARY EMPHASES
OF JESUS' MIRACLES

SHOW MERCY
50%

DELIVER
25%

CONFIRM DIETY
22%

JUDGE
3%

9 Healings from **Sickness**

8 Healings from **Disability**

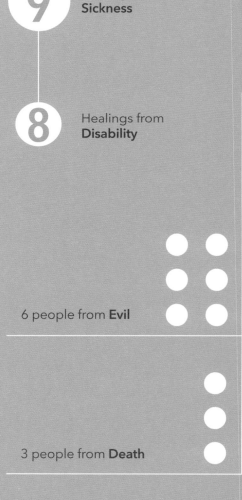

6 people from **Evil**

3 people from **Death**

*Numbers differ from scholar to scholar.

OVER

10,000

PEOPLE FED

At least

39

Miracles
Performed
by Jesus

5,000+
Matthew 14:14-21

4,000+
Mark 8:1-9

WHERE DID JESUS PERFORM MIRACLES?**

Named Location	Number of Miracles	
Capernaum		10
Sea of Galilee		4
The Decapolis		4
Jerusalem		3
Galilee		2
Bethany		2
Cana		1
Nain		1
Tyre and Sidon		1
Caesarea		1
Jericho		1
Samaria		1
Gethsemane		1

**Not all miracles have a named location, while other named locations lie within a wider region. This chart gives an interesting general look at the places where Jesus performed miracles.

06

Grace Day

Take this day as an
opportunity to catch up on
your reading, pray, and rest
in the presence of the Lord.

Mark 11:22-23

JESUS REPLIED TO THEM, "HAVE FAITH IN GOD.
I ASSURE YOU: IF ANYONE SAYS TO THIS MOUNTAIN,
'BE LIFTED UP AND THROWN INTO THE SEA,' AND
DOES NOT DOUBT IN HIS HEART, BUT BELIEVES
THAT WHAT HE SAYS WILL HAPPEN, IT WILL BE
DONE FOR HIM."

Weekly Truth

Memorizing Scripture is one of the best ways to carry God-breathed truth, instruction, and reproof wherever we go.

As we study the miracles of Jesus, we remember that even our very salvation is impossible apart from Him, and that He is the source of all things.

BUT JESUS LOOKED AT THEM AND SAID,
"WITH MEN THIS IS IMPOSSIBLE, BUT WITH GOD

all things

ARE POSSIBLE."

MATTHEW 19:26

Christ Overcomes Evil

Jesus casts out demons

Luke 8:27-39 📖 *Also appears in Matthew 8:28-34 and Mark 5:1-15*

27 When He got out on land, a demon-possessed man from the town met Him. For a long time he had worn no clothes and did not stay in a house but in the tombs. 28 When he saw Jesus, he cried out, fell down before Him, and said in a loud voice, "What do You have to do with me, Jesus, You Son of the Most High God? I beg You, don't torment me!" 29 For He had commanded the unclean spirit to come out of the man. Many times it had seized him, and though he was guarded, bound by chains and shackles, he would snap the restraints and be driven by the demon into deserted places.

30 "What is your name?" Jesus asked him.

"Legion," he said—because many demons had entered him. 31 And they begged Him not to banish them to the abyss.

32 A large herd of pigs was there, feeding on the hillside. The demons begged Him to permit them to enter the pigs, and He gave them permission. 33 The demons came out of the man and entered the pigs, and the herd rushed down the steep bank into the lake and drowned. 34 When the men who tended them saw what had happened, they ran off and reported it in the town and in the countryside. 35 Then people went out to see what had happened. They came to Jesus and found the man the demons had departed from, sitting at Jesus' feet, dressed and in his right mind. And they were afraid. 36 Meanwhile, the eyewitnesses reported to them how the demon-possessed man was delivered. 37 Then all the people of the Gerasene region asked Him to leave them, because they were gripped by great fear. So getting into the boat, He returned.

38 The man from whom the demons had departed kept begging Him to be with Him. But He sent him away and said, 39 "Go back to your home, and tell all that God has done for you." And off he went, proclaiming throughout the town all that Jesus had done for him.

Matthew 9:32-34

DRIVING OUT A DEMON

[32] Just as they were going out, a demon-possessed man who was unable to speak was brought to Him. [33] When the demon had been driven out, the man spoke. And the crowds were amazed, saying,

"Nothing like this has ever been seen in Israel!"

[34] But the Pharisees said, "He drives out demons by the ruler of the demons!"

Luke 11:14 *Also appears in Matthew 12:22-23*

Now He was driving out a demon that was mute. When the demon came out, the man who had been mute, spoke, and the crowds were amazed.

Mark 7:24-30 *Also appears in Matthew 15:21-28*

A GENTILE MOTHER'S FAITH

²⁴ He got up and departed from there to the region of Tyre and Sidon. He entered a house and did not want anyone to know it, but He could not escape notice. ²⁵ Instead, immediately after hearing about Him, a woman whose little daughter had an unclean spirit came and fell at His feet. ²⁶ Now the woman was Greek, a Syrophoenician by birth, and she kept asking Him to drive the demon out of her daughter. ²⁷ He said to her, "Allow the children to be satisfied first, because it isn't right to take the children's bread and throw it to the dogs."

²⁸ But she replied to Him, "Lord, even the dogs under the table eat the children's crumbs."

²⁹ Then He told her, "Because of this reply, you may go. The demon has gone out of your daughter." ³⁰ When she went back to her home, she found her child lying on the bed, and the demon was gone.

Luke 4:31-37 *Also appears in Mark 1:21-28*

DRIVING OUT AN UNCLEAN SPIRIT

³¹ Then He went down to Capernaum, a town in Galilee, and was teaching them on the Sabbath. ³² They were astonished at His teaching because His message had authority. ³³ In the synagogue there was a man with an unclean demonic spirit who cried out with a loud voice, ³⁴ "Leave us alone! What do You have to do with us, Jesus—Nazarene? Have You come to destroy us? I know who You are—the Holy One of God!"

³⁵ But Jesus rebuked him and said, "Be quiet and come out of him!"

And throwing him down before them, the demon came out of him without hurting him at all. ³⁶ Amazement came over them all, and they kept saying to one another, "What is this message? For He commands the unclean spirits with authority and power, and they come out!" ³⁷ And news about Him began to go out to every place in the vicinity.

Matthew 17:14-21 📖 *Also appears in Mark 9:17-29 and Luke 9:38-43*

THE POWER OF FAITH OVER A DEMON

[14] When they reached the crowd, a man approached and knelt down before Him. [15] "Lord," he said, "have mercy on my son, because he has seizures and suffers severely. He often falls into the fire and often into the water. [16] I brought him to Your disciples, but they couldn't heal him."

[17] Jesus replied, "You unbelieving and rebellious generation! How long will I be with you? How long must I put up with you? Bring him here to Me." [18] Then Jesus rebuked the demon, and it came out of him, and from that moment the boy was healed.

[19] Then the disciples approached Jesus privately and said, "Why couldn't we drive it out?"

[20] "Because of your little faith," He told them. "For I assure you: If you have faith the size of a mustard seed, you will tell this mountain, 'Move from here to there,' and it will move. Nothing will be impossible for you. [[21] However, this kind does not come out except by prayer and fasting.]"*

Some manuscripts omit bracketed text.

How did Jesus drive out demons?

What did the Pharisees think of Jesus' miracles? Why?

How did Jesus free the Canaanite woman's daughter?

How did Jesus respond when the disciples asked why they were unable to drive out the demon from the boy in Matthew 17?

NOTES

Christ
Gives Sight

Jesus heals the man born blind

John 9

THE SIXTH SIGN: HEALING A MAN BORN BLIND

[1] As He was passing by, He saw a man blind from birth. [2] His disciples questioned Him: "Rabbi, who sinned, this man or his parents, that he was born blind?"

[3] "Neither this man nor his parents sinned," Jesus answered. "This came about so that God's works might be displayed in him.

[4] We must do the works of Him who sent Me while it is day. Night is coming when no one can work. [5] As long as I am in the world, I am the light of the world."

[6] After He said these things He spit on the ground, made some mud from the saliva, and spread the mud on his eyes. [7] "Go," He told him, "wash in the pool of Siloam" (which means "Sent"). So he left, washed, and came back seeing.

[8] His neighbors and those who formerly had seen him as a beggar said, "Isn't this the man who sat begging?" [9] Some said, "He's the one." "No," others were saying, "but he looks like him."

He kept saying, "I'm the one!"

[10] Therefore they asked him, "Then how were your eyes opened?"

[11] He answered, "The man called Jesus made mud, spread it on my eyes, and told me, 'Go to Siloam and wash.' So when I went and washed I received my sight."

[12] "Where is He?" they asked.

"I don't know," he said.

THE HEALED MAN'S TESTIMONY

¹³ They brought the man who used to be blind to the Pharisees. ¹⁴ The day that Jesus made the mud and opened his eyes was a Sabbath. ¹⁵ So again the Pharisees asked him how he received his sight.

"He put mud on my eyes," he told them. "I washed and I can see."

¹⁶ Therefore some of the Pharisees said, "This man is not from God, for He doesn't keep the Sabbath!" But others were saying, "How can a sinful man perform such signs?" And there was a division among them.

¹⁷ Again they asked the blind man, "What do you say about Him, since He opened your eyes?"

"He's a prophet," he said.

¹⁸ The Jews did not believe this about him—that he was blind and received sight—until they summoned the parents of the one who had received his sight.

¹⁹ They asked them, "Is this your son, the one you say was born blind? How then does he now see?"

²⁰ "We know this is our son and that he was born blind," his parents answered. ²¹ "But we don't know how he now sees, and we don't know who opened his eyes. Ask him; he's of age. He will speak for himself." ²² His parents said these things because they were afraid of the Jews, since the Jews had already agreed that if anyone confessed Him as Messiah, he would be banned from the synagogue. ²³ This is why his parents said, "He's of age; ask him."

²⁴ So a second time they summoned the man who had been blind and told him, "Give glory to God. We know that this man is a sinner!"

²⁵ He answered, "Whether or not He's a sinner, I don't know. One thing I do know: I was blind, and now I can see!"

²⁶ Then they asked him, "What did He do to you? How did He open your eyes?"

²⁷ "I already told you," he said, "and you didn't listen. Why do you want to hear it again? You don't want to become His disciples too, do you?"

²⁸ They ridiculed him: "You're that man's disciple, but we're Moses' disciples. ²⁹ We know that God has spoken to Moses. But this man—we don't know where He's from!"

³⁰ "This is an amazing thing," the man told them. "You don't know where He is from, yet He opened my eyes! ³¹ We know that God doesn't listen to sinners, but if anyone is God-fearing and does His will, He listens to him. ³² Throughout history no one has ever heard of someone opening the eyes of a person born blind. ³³ If this man were not from God, He wouldn't be able to do anything."

³⁴ "You were born entirely in sin," they replied, "and are you trying to teach us?" Then they threw him out.

THE BLIND MAN'S SIGHT AND THE PHARISEES' BLINDNESS

³⁵ When Jesus heard that they had thrown the man out, He found him and asked, "Do you believe in the Son of Man?"

³⁶ "Who is He, Sir, that I may believe in Him?" he asked.

³⁷ Jesus answered, "You have seen Him; in fact, He is the One speaking with you."

³⁸ "I believe, Lord!" he said, and he worshiped Him.

³⁹ Jesus said, "I came into this world for judgment, in order that those who do not see will see and those who do see will become blind."

⁴⁰ Some of the Pharisees who were with Him heard these things and asked Him, "We aren't blind too, are we?"

⁴¹ "If you were blind," Jesus told them, "you wouldn't have sin. But now that you say, 'We see'—your sin remains."

"I came into this world for judgment, in order that those who do not see will see and those who do see will become blind."

**Jesus heals
two blind men
by touching
their eyes**

Matthew 9:27-31

HEALING THE BLIND

²⁷ As Jesus went on from there, two blind men followed Him, shouting, "Have mercy on us, Son of David!"

²⁸ When He entered the house, the blind men approached Him, and Jesus said to them, "Do you believe that I can do this?"

"Yes, Lord," they answered Him.

²⁹ Then He touched their eyes, saying, "Let it be done for you according to your faith!" ³⁰ And their eyes were opened. Then Jesus warned them sternly, "Be sure that no one finds out!" ³¹ But they went out and spread the news about Him throughout that whole area.

**Jesus heals
Bartimaeus**

Mark 10:46-52 *Also appears in Matthew 20:29-34 and Luke 18:35-43*

A BLIND MAN HEALED

⁴⁶ They came to Jericho. And as He was leaving Jericho with His disciples and a large crowd, Bartimaeus (the son of Timaeus), a blind beggar, was sitting by the road. ⁴⁷ When he heard that it was Jesus the Nazarene, he began to cry out, "Son of David, Jesus, have mercy on me!" ⁴⁸ Many people told him to keep quiet, but he was crying out all the more, "Have mercy on me, Son of David!"

⁴⁹ Jesus stopped and said, "Call him."

So they called the blind man and said to him, "Have courage! Get up; He's calling for you." ⁵⁰ He threw off his coat, jumped up, and came to Jesus.

⁵¹ Then Jesus answered him, "What do you want Me to do for you?"

"Rabbouni," the blind man told Him, "I want to see!"

⁵² "Go your way," Jesus told him. "Your faith has healed you." Immediately he could see and began to follow Him on the road.

Why does Scripture tell us the man in John 9 was born blind? What is the significance of that detail?

What did Jesus do to heal the two blind men in Matthew 9? How did they respond?

Consider the imagery of darkness and light. How is deliverance from blindness a metaphor for the light of hope and understanding that faith in Christ brings?

NOTES

Christ Restores Broken Bodies

Jesus heals a paralyzed man lowered through a roof

Luke 5:18-26 📖 *Also appears in Matthew 9:2-7 and Mark 2:3-12*

[18] Just then some men came, carrying on a mat a man who was paralyzed. They tried to bring him in and set him down before Him. [19] Since they could not find a way to bring him in because of the crowd, they went up on the roof and lowered him on the mat through the roof tiles into the middle of the crowd before Jesus.

[20] Seeing their faith He said, "Friend, your sins are forgiven you."

[21] Then the scribes and the Pharisees began to think: "Who is this man who speaks blasphemies? Who can forgive sins but God alone?"

[22] But perceiving their thoughts, Jesus replied to them, "Why are you thinking this in your hearts? [23] Which is easier: to say, 'Your sins are forgiven you,' or to say, 'Get up and walk'? [24] But so you may know that the Son of Man has authority on earth to forgive sins"—He told the paralyzed man, "I tell you: Get up, pick up your mat, and go home."

[25] Immediately he got up before them, picked up what he had been lying on, and went home glorifying God. [26] Then everyone was astounded, and they were giving glory to God. And they were filled with awe and said, "We have seen incredible things today!"

Jesus heals the man with the withered hand

Matthew 12:10-13 📖 *Also appears in Mark 3:1-5 and Luke 6:6-11*

[10] There He saw a man who had a paralyzed hand. And in order to accuse Him they asked Him, "Is it lawful to heal on the Sabbath?"

[11] But He said to them, "What man among you, if he had a sheep that fell into a pit on the Sabbath, wouldn't take hold of it and lift it out? [12] A man is worth far more than a sheep, so it is lawful to do what is good on the Sabbath."

[13] Then He told the man, "Stretch out your hand." So he stretched it out, and it was restored, as good as the other.

Jesus heals the crippled woman

Luke 13:10-17

HEALING A DAUGHTER OF ABRAHAM

[10] As He was teaching in one of the synagogues on the Sabbath, [11] a woman was there who had been disabled by a spirit for over 18 years. She was bent over and could not straighten up at all. [12] When Jesus saw her, He called out to her, "Woman, you are free of your disability." [13] Then He laid His hands on her, and instantly she was restored and began to glorify God.

[14] But the leader of the synagogue, indignant because Jesus had healed on the Sabbath, responded by telling the crowd, "There are six days when work should be done; therefore come on those days and be healed and not on the Sabbath day."

[15] But the Lord answered him and said, "Hypocrites! Doesn't each one of you untie his ox or donkey from the feeding trough on the Sabbath and lead it to water? [16] Satan has bound this woman, a daughter of Abraham, for 18 years—shouldn't she be untied from this bondage on the Sabbath day?"

[17] When He had said these things, all His adversaries were humiliated, but the whole crowd was rejoicing over all the glorious things He was doing.

Jesus heals the paralyzed man at the pool of Bethesda

John 5:1-15

THE THIRD SIGN: HEALING THE SICK

[1] After this, a Jewish festival took place, and Jesus went up to Jerusalem. [2] By the Sheep Gate in Jerusalem there is a pool, called Bethesda in Hebrew, which has five colonnades. [3] Within these lay a large number of the sick—blind, lame, and paralyzed [—waiting for the moving of the water, [4] because an angel would go down into the pool from time to time and stir up the water. Then the first one who got in after the water was stirred up recovered from whatever ailment he had].*

[5] One man was there who had been sick for 38 years. [6] When Jesus saw him lying there and knew he had already been there a long time, He said to him, "Do you want to get well?"

[7] "Sir," the sick man answered, "I don't have a man to put me into the pool when the water is stirred up, but while I'm coming, someone goes down ahead of me."

[8] "Get up," Jesus told him, "pick up your mat and walk!" [9] Instantly the man got well, picked up his mat, and started to walk.

Now that day was the Sabbath, [10] so the Jews said to the man who had been healed, "This is the Sabbath! It's illegal for you to pick up your mat."

[11] He replied, "The man who made me well told me, 'Pick up your mat and walk.'"

[12] "Who is this man who told you, 'Pick up your mat and walk'?" they asked. [13] But the man who was cured did not know who it was, because Jesus had slipped away into the crowd that was there.

[14] After this, Jesus found him in the temple complex and said to him, "See, you are well. Do not sin anymore, so that something worse doesn't happen to you." [15] The man went and reported to the Jews that it was Jesus who had made him well.

* Some manuscripts omit bracketed text.

What did Jesus do first when the men lowered the paralyzed man through the roof? What does this teach us?

What did Jesus do in each of these passages that resulted in healing?

Read Genesis 1 and John 1. What is the significance of words that come from the mouth of God?

NOTES

All Hail the Power of Jesus' Name

TEXT: Edward Perronet, 1780

TUNE: Oliver Holden, 1793

Christ Heals
Illness and Injury

Jesus heals a man with leprosy

Mark 1:40-45 📖 *Also appears in Matthew 8:1-4 and Luke 5:12-14*

A MAN CLEANSED

⁴⁰ Then a man with a serious skin disease came to Him and, on his knees, begged Him: "If You are willing, You can make me clean."

⁴¹ Moved with compassion, Jesus reached out His hand and touched him. "I am willing," He told him. "Be made clean." ⁴² Immediately the disease left him, and he was healed. ⁴³ Then He sternly warned him and sent him away at once, ⁴⁴ telling him, "See that you say nothing to anyone; but go and show yourself to the priest, and offer what Moses prescribed for your cleansing, as a testimony to them." ⁴⁵ Yet he went out and began to proclaim it widely and to spread the news, with the result that Jesus could no longer enter a town openly. But He was out in deserted places, and they would come to Him from everywhere.

Jesus heals Peter's mother-in-law from a fever

Matthew 8:14-15 📖 *Also appears in Mark 1:30-3 and Luke 4:38-39*

HEALINGS AT CAPERNAUM

¹⁴ When Jesus went into Peter's house, He saw his mother-in-law lying in bed with a fever. ¹⁵ So He touched her hand, and the fever left her. Then she got up and began to serve Him.

Jesus heals the man with dropsy on the Sabbath

Luke 14:1-4

A SABBATH CONTROVERSY

¹ One Sabbath, when He went to eat at the house of one of the leading Pharisees, they were watching Him closely. ² There in front of Him was a man whose body was swollen with fluid. ³ In response, Jesus asked the law experts and the Pharisees, "Is it lawful to heal on the Sabbath or not?" ⁴ But they kept silent. He took the man, healed him, and sent him away.

Jesus heals the high priest's servant's ear

Luke 22:50-51

⁵⁰ Then one of them struck the high priest's slave and cut off his right ear.

⁵¹ But Jesus responded, "No more of this!" And touching his ear, He healed him.

Jesus heals the nobleman's son

John 4:46-54

THE SECOND SIGN: HEALING AN OFFICIAL'S SON

⁴⁶ Then He went again to Cana of Galilee, where He had turned the water into wine. There was a certain royal official whose son was ill at Capernaum. ⁴⁷ When this man heard that Jesus had come from Judea into Galilee, he went to Him and pleaded with Him to come down and heal his son, for he was about to die.

⁴⁸ Jesus told him, "Unless you people see signs and wonders, you will not believe."

⁴⁹ "Sir," the official said to Him, "come down before my boy dies!"

⁵⁰ "Go," Jesus told him, "your son will live." The man believed what Jesus said to him and departed.

⁵¹ While he was still going down, his slaves met him saying that his boy was alive. ⁵² He asked them at what time he got better. "Yesterday at seven in the morning the fever left him," they answered. ⁵³ The father realized this was the very hour at which Jesus had told him, "Your son will live." Then he himself believed, along with his whole household.

⁵⁴ This, therefore, was the second sign Jesus performed after He came from Judea to Galilee.

Why did Jesus touch the man with leprosy?

What was Peter's mother-in-law's response when Jesus healed her?

Why did Jesus heal the man with dropsy on the Sabbath?

How did Jesus heal the nobleman's son?

NOTES

Christ Conquers Death

Jesus raises
Jairus's
daughter from
the dead

Matthew 9:18-26 📖 *Also appears in Mark 5:21-43 and Luke 8:40-56*

A GIRL RESTORED AND A WOMAN HEALED

¹⁸ As He was telling them these things, suddenly one of the leaders came and knelt down before Him, saying, "My daughter is near death, but come and lay Your hand on her, and she will live." ¹⁹ So Jesus and His disciples got up and followed him.

²⁰ Just then, a woman who had suffered from bleeding for 12 years approached from behind and touched the tassel on His robe, ²¹ for she said to herself, "If I can just touch His robe, I'll be made well!"

²² But Jesus turned and saw her.

"Have courage, daughter,"

He said. "Your faith has made you well." And the woman was made well from that moment.

²³ When Jesus came to the leader's house, He saw the flute players and a crowd lamenting loudly. ²⁴ "Leave," He said, "because the girl isn't dead, but sleeping." And they started laughing at Him. ²⁵ But when the crowd had been put outside, He went in and took her by the hand, and the girl got up. ²⁶ And this news spread throughout that whole area.

Jesus raises
the widow
of Nain's son
from the dead

Luke 7:11-17

A WIDOW'S SON RAISED TO LIFE

[11] Soon afterward He was on His way to a town called Nain. His disciples and a large crowd were traveling with Him. [12] Just as He neared the gate of the town, a dead man was being carried out. He was his mother's only son, and she was a widow. A large crowd from the city was also with her. [13] When the Lord saw her, He had compassion on her and said, "Don't cry." [14] Then He came up and touched the open coffin, and the pallbearers stopped. And He said, "Young man, I tell you, get up!"

[15] The dead man sat up and began to speak, and Jesus gave him to his mother. [16] Then fear came over everyone, and they glorified God, saying, "A great prophet has risen among us," and "God has visited His people." [17] This report about Him went throughout Judea and all the vicinity.

Jesus raises
his friend
Lazarus from
the dead

John 11:17-44

THE RESURRECTION AND THE LIFE

[17] When Jesus arrived, He found that Lazarus had already been in the tomb four days. [18] Bethany was near Jerusalem (about two miles away). [19] Many of the Jews had come to Martha and Mary to comfort them about their brother. [20] As soon as Martha heard that Jesus was coming, she went to meet Him. But Mary remained seated in the house.

[21] Then Martha said to Jesus, "Lord, if You had been here, my brother wouldn't have died. [22] Yet even now I know that whatever You ask from God, God will give You."

[23] "Your brother will rise again," Jesus told her.

[24] Martha said, "I know that he will rise again in the resurrection at the last day."

[25] Jesus said to her, "I am the resurrection and the life. The one who believes in Me, even if he dies, will live. [26] Everyone who lives and believes in Me will never die—ever. Do you believe this?"

[27] "Yes, Lord," she told Him, "I believe You are the Messiah, the Son of God, who comes into the world."

"I am the resurrection and the life. The one who believes in Me, even if he dies, will live. Everyone who lives and believes in Me will never die— ever. Do you believe this?"

JESUS SHARES THE SORROW OF DEATH

[28] Having said this, she went back and called her sister Mary, saying in private, "The Teacher is here and is calling for you."

[29] As soon as she heard this, she got up quickly and went to Him. [30] Jesus had not yet come into the village but was still in the place where Martha had met Him. [31] The Jews who were with her in the house consoling her saw that Mary got up quickly and went out. So they followed her, supposing that she was going to the tomb to cry there.

[32] When Mary came to where Jesus was and saw Him, she fell at His feet and told Him, "Lord, if You had been here, my brother would not have died!"

[33] When Jesus saw her crying, and the Jews who had come with her crying, He was angry in His spirit and deeply moved. [34] "Where have you put him?" He asked.

"Lord," they told Him, "come and see."

[35] Jesus wept.

[36] So the Jews said, "See how He loved him!" [37] But some of them said, "Couldn't He who opened the blind man's eyes also have kept this man from dying?"

THE SEVENTH SIGN: RAISING LAZARUS FROM THE DEAD

[38] Then Jesus, angry in Himself again, came to the tomb. It was a cave, and a stone was lying against it. [39] "Remove the stone," Jesus said.

Martha, the dead man's sister, told Him, "Lord, he's already decaying. It's been four days."

[40] Jesus said to her, "Didn't I tell you that if you believed you would see the glory of God?"

[41] So they removed the stone. Then Jesus raised His eyes and said, "Father, I thank You that You heard Me. [42] I know that You always hear Me, but because of the crowd standing here I said this, so they may believe You sent Me." [43] After He said this, He shouted with a loud voice, "Lazarus, come out!" [44] The dead man came out bound hand and foot with linen strips and with his face wrapped in a cloth. Jesus said to them, "Loose him and let him go."

Jesus stopped on His way to heal Jairus's daughter. What does this teach us about Him?

Why did Jesus raise the widow's son?

How is Jesus' resurrection of Lazarus a foreshadowing of His own resurrection?

NOTES

13

Grace Day

Take this day as an
opportunity to catch up on
your reading, pray, and rest
in the presence of the Lord.

Ephesians 3:20-21

NOW TO HIM WHO IS ABLE TO DO ABOVE AND
BEYOND ALL THAT WE ASK OR THINK ACCORDING
TO THE POWER THAT WORKS IN US—TO HIM BE
GLORY IN THE CHURCH AND IN CHRIST JESUS TO
ALL GENERATIONS, FOREVER AND EVER. AMEN.

Weekly Truth

Memorizing Scripture is one of the best ways to carry God-breathed truth, instruction, and reproof wherever we go.

As we study the miracles of Jesus, we remember that He fulfilled the prophecies of the Old Testament, displaying His divinity in mighty and merciful ways.

YOU ARE THE GOD WHO WORKS

YOU HAVE MADE KNOWN YOUR
STRENGTH AMONG THE PEOPLES.

PSALM 77:14 NASB

Where did I study?

○ HOME   ○ OFFICE   ○ COFFEE SHOP
○ CHURCH   ○ A FRIEND'S HOUSE   ○ OTHER

DID I LISTEN TO MUSIC?

ARTIST:

SONG:

SCRIPTURE I WILL
SHARE WITH A FRIEND:

WHEN DID I HAVE MY BEST STUDYING SUCCESS?

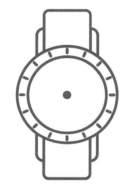

WHAT WAS HAPPENING IN THE WORLD?

What was my best takeaway?

WHAT WAS MY BIGGEST FEAR?

▷

What was my greatest comfort?

_____
_____
_____
_____
_____

I LEARNED THESE UNEXPECTED NEW THINGS:

1

2

3

END DATE

| MONTH | DAY | YEAR |

COLOPHON

This book was printed offset in Nashville, Tennessee, on 80# Lynx Opaque. Typefaces used include Avenir, Garamond, and Euclid. Cover is printed offset on 12 pt Saturn C1S with a soft-touch matte laminate. Finished size is 8"x10".

EDITORS-IN-CHIEF: Raechel Myers and Amanda Bible Williams

MANAGING EDITOR: Rebecca Faires

EDITORS: Russ Ramsey and Kara Gause

CREATIVE DIRECTOR: Ryan Myers

ART DIRECTOR: Amanda Barnhart

LETTERING: Cymone Wilder

PRODUCTION DESIGN: Kelsea Allen

THEOLOGICAL OVERSIGHT:
Russ Ramsey, MDiv., ThM.
and Nate Shurden, MDiv.

COMMUNITY CORRESPONDENT: Kaitlin Wernet

COVER PHOTOGRAPHER: Melissa Hope

PHOTOGRAPHY: Melissa Hope, Kellie Beth Scott, and Alyssa Valletta

EDITORIAL INTERN: Ellen Taylor

SUBSCRIPTION INQUIRIES:
orders@shereadstruth.com

She Reads Truth is a worldwide community of women who read God's Word together every day.

Founded in 2012, She Reads Truth invites women of all ages to engage with Scripture through daily reading plans, online conversation led by a vibrant community of contributors, and offline resources created at the intersection of beauty, goodness, and Truth.

STOP BY

shereadstruth.com

SHOP

shopshereadstruth.com

KEEP IN TOUCH

@shereadstruth

DOWNLOAD THE APP

SEND A NOTE

hello@shereadstruth.com

CONNECT

#SheReadsTruth

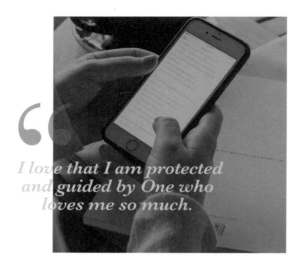

I love that I am protected and guided by One who loves me so much.

Beauty

The She Reads Truth **comments section** is one of our favorite places on the internet. There, on the She Reads Truth app or shereadstruth.com, you're always sure to find encouragement from a diverse community of women who love God's Word. Here's a recent comment from Day 12 of the John study from Deb, a fellow She: "I so love the visual of Jesus as the good shepherd, tenderly caring for His unruly flock. I love that I am protected and guided by One who loves me so much. I am the best me when I stay in His pasture—a safe and ever-satisfying pasture."

Goodness

If you're looking for a simple way to add a little goodness to your day, consider giving *The Happy Hour with Jamie Ivey* podcast a try. Like a girls night with best friends, Jamie talks about both the big and small things in life with guests you're sure to love. Start with **episode 110** to hear Jamie's interview with our very own Amanda Bible Williams!

THE *happy Hour* with JAMIE IVEY

We've been learning all kinds of fun facts around the #SRThq lunch table this week. After implementing an informal **"Lunch & Learn"** conversation starter, we've taken turns teaching the rest of the team about a topic of choice. Just this week, we covered chaga mushrooms, astronaut fashion, car parts, and tap dancing! Need to know about the ins and outs of the shim sham? Say no more. We'll meet you in the conference room, where our current favorite quote is scrawled on the whiteboard. It's from Alfred Lord Tennyson: "Bible reading is an education in itself."

 SEND A NOTE   hello@shereadstruth.com

& Truth